GOD'S PROMISE KEPT

Short daily devotionals for Advent

by Sarah Tummey

Published by JJ Moffs Independent Book Publisher 2020

JJ Moffs Independent Book Publisher Ltd
Grove House Farm, Grovewood Road,
Misterton, Nottinghamshire DN10 4EF

Typeset and cover design by Anna Richards

To Alan and Jill, Leston and Sarah, Pete and Carol, Neil and Kate. Without you speaking God's Word into my life, I'm sure this book would never have come into being. Thank you.

INTRODUCTION

"At that time people will say, 'Our God is doing this! We have waited for Him, and He has come to save us'" – Isaiah 25:9

The first thirty-nine books of the Bible (known to Christians as the Old Testament) transport us from creation to the time of Jesus' birth. At Christmas, we celebrate Jesus being born, but sometimes not much is said about events leading up to that moment. I have a real love of the Old Testament, its many characters, and how God spoke to them about His Son before He was even born. For example, He said to Isaiah: "At that time people will say, 'Our God is doing this! We have waited for Him, and He has come to save us'" (Isaiah 25:9). Let's focus on one Old Testament reading every day until 25 December. Hopefully it will enrich our celebration of Christmas, as we see that Jesus - this ruler of nations, born in the small town of Bethlehem – is God's promise kept.

When I wrote this series of Advent readings, what I wanted more than anything was for it to be accessible. I've deliberately kept the reflections short so that even on a busy day, you can fit in the day's Bible-reading alongside my words. I hope you come away with an understanding of the backstory of Christmas, and a love of God's story as a whole.

Unless otherwise stated, all Scripture quotations are taken from the Holy Bible: New Century Version.
Those marked NKJV are from the New King James Version.
ERV = Easy to Read Version.
Those marked NIV are from the Holy Bible: New International Version.

1 DECEMBER
God's Plan
Genesis 3:9-15

"I will make you and the woman enemies to each other. Your descendants and her descendants will be enemies. One of her descendants will crush your head, and you will bite His heel"
- Genesis 3:15

This Advent journey starts out with the very first question in the Bible – a question from God to Adam: "Where are you?" Adam was the first man to be created, and where was he in terms of his connection with God? He was hiding – hiding because he disobeyed the one command God had given him, and ate from the tree he wasn't supposed to eat from. Because of that disobedience, wrongdoing and its consequences entered our world. So did the need to be saved from that wrongdoing, but God wasn't surprised. He already had a plan.

In Genesis 3:15, God hints at discord between those who belong to the serpent (the devil), and those who've put their faith in Jesus. The devil is against Christians, but ultimately, Jesus will crush the devil's head. "Christ had no sin, but God made Him become sin so that in Christ we could become right with God" (2 Corinthians 5:21).

This happened on the cross when those nails through His feet literally bit into His heel. His words "It is finished" (John 19:30) showed that everything necessary had now been done; God's plan was accomplished. From Jesus' death until the end of time, people continue to put their faith in Him and His finished work on the cross. "But as many as received Him, to them He gave the right to become children of God" (John 1:12, NKJV).

I'm so glad God knew our need, and had a plan to fulfil it — a descendant of Eve, hundreds of years into the future, born to be our Saviour.

2 December
A Promised Priest
Psalm 110:1-4

"The LORD has made a promise and will not change His mind. He said, 'You are a priest forever, a priest like Melchizedek'" - Psalm 110:4

This is King David with a message about the Christ, but who was Melchizedek, and why is it important to have a priest like him?

Melchizedek was a bit of a mystery – "without father, without mother, without genealogy, having neither beginning of days nor end of life" (Hebrews 7:3, NKJV). We first come across him in Genesis 14:18-20. Several generations after Adam came a man called Abram. He was returning from rescuing his nephew (who'd been captured) when Melchizedek, a priest for God Most High, came out to meet him. He brought bread and wine and blessed Abram, praising God for helping him defeat his enemies. Then Abram gave him a tenth of all he had brought back from the battle.

Abram's name changed to Abraham and his grandson Jacob had twelve sons, two of them being Levi and Judah. The very first priests were Aaron and his sons, who descended from Levi. "Pouring oil on them will make them a family of priests, they and their descendants from now on" (Exodus 40:15), but there was a problem. "No one could be made spiritually perfect through that system of priests. So, there was a need for another priest to come" (Hebrews 7:11, ERV).

The explanation continues. Jesus came from the family of Judah, and "Moses said nothing about priests belonging to that tribe. He was not made a priest by human rules and laws but through the power of His life, which continues forever. When one of the other priests died, he could not continue being a priest. So there were many priests. But because Jesus lives forever, He will never stop serving as priest. So He is able always to save those who come to God through Him" (Hebrews 7:14, 16, 23-25)

When one system couldn't make us perfect, God gave us a better one, with His Son as the everlasting Priest.

3 DECEMBER
A Lamb Provided
Genesis 22:1-14

"Abraham answered, 'God will give us the lamb for the sacrifice, my son'" – Genesis 22:8

This story is all about priorities. God asks Abraham to take his son Isaac, the only son of his wife Sarah, and give him as an offering to God – kill him, in other words. This must have devastated him, but God ruled Abraham's life, so he set off with his son to do the deed. As they went, Isaac had a question. "We have the fire and the wood, but where is the lamb we will burn as a sacrifice?" Abraham assured him God would provide a lamb (Genesis 22:8).

Of course, God wouldn't endorse the loss of a human life in this way. Once Abraham had passed the test, proving he wouldn't keep anything back from God (including his beloved son), Isaac was spared. Abraham looked up and saw a ram caught in some greenery, which he used as his offering – a ram, not a lamb. The lamb would come later.

Skip forward several hundred years, and perhaps you know the story of God rescuing Israel from her slavery in Egypt (Exodus 3-12). The pharaoh wouldn't let Israel go, resulting in several disasters. They were finally allowed to leave after the firstborn son of every Egyptian was killed. The night it happened, Israel had a Passover meal. They ate a lamb and put its blood on the doorposts of their houses, so God's disaster would pass over them and their families would be safe.

But that again was pointing us to a time further into the future when Jesus, who was called the Lamb of God (John 1:29), was killed on our behalf. His blood was shed on a cross. When we put our faith in Him and accept He died in our place, God's punishment passes over us and we too are safe.

Isaac's life was spared, and Abraham named the place The LORD Provides (Genesis 22:13-14). Many centuries later, Jesus trudged painfully to a cross, giving Himself so we could be saved from death and brought into everlasting life.

4 December
Israel's Rock
Exodus 17:6-13

"'I will stand in front of you on a rock at Mount Sinai. Hit that rock with the stick, and water will come out of it so that the people can drink'" – Exodus 17:6

These few verses relate two instances involving rocks. God caused water to come out of a rock, and Moses sat on a rock with friends holding his arms up so Israel would win their battle. On the face of it, they seem to have little to do with Jesus, but Paul says otherwise.

In a letter to the early church at Corinth, Paul talks about their ancestors who followed Moses. "They all ate the same spiritual food, and all drank the same spiritual drink. They drank from that spiritual rock that followed them, and that rock was Christ" (1 Corinthians 10:3-4). In a wonderful way that probably none of the Israelites understood at the time, eating that manna God gave them from heaven (Exodus 16:14-31) and drinking the water He brought out of the rock connected them to Jesus.

Jesus called Himself the true bread from heaven. "I tell you the truth, it was not Moses who gave you bread from heaven; it is My Father who is giving you the true bread from heaven. God's bread is the One who comes down from heaven and gives life to the world" (John 6:32-33). Jesus gives life. He nourishes, and He also said faith in Him would produce rivers of living water (John 7:37-39).

When His friend Peter confesses Jesus is the Christ – the Son of the living God, Jesus tells him: "On this rock I will build My church" (Matthew 16:16-18). Are we building our lives on the foundation that Jesus is the Christ?

I think we're a bit like the Israelites. If we look at our history with the benefit of hindsight, we can probably see ways God was involved, even if we didn't always know it. Can we stop for a few minutes today and just think back over our lives, thanking God for His involvement – the things He's protected us from, or helped us with? I'm sure He'll enjoy hearing from us.

5 December
A Star and a Sceptre
Numbers 24:15-19

"A star will come from Jacob; a ruler will rise from Israel" –
Numbers 24:17

Moses has led the Israelites out of Egypt. They're camping beside the Jordan River, on the flatlands of Moab, but the king of Moab saw how they defeated another enemy and he and his nation are terrified of them. That's why he sends for Balaam – a man who used magic to get messages from God.

King Balak said to Balaam: "Come and put a curse on them. Maybe then I can defeat them and make them leave the area. I know that if you bless someone, the blessings happen, and if you put a curse on someone, it happens" (Numbers 22:6), but God didn't want Balaam to curse Israel – the nation He had blessed. He was so angry that He sent an angel to block his way and even made a donkey talk, but you can read about that later.

The point here is that King Balak wanted Balaam to curse Israel, but when the messages came from God, he ended up blessing them instead. When he saw what was happening, we're told he stopped using magic as before. Then the Spirit of God came on him (Numbers 24:1-2). When someone's speaking through the Spirit, you know what they say will be really important.

That's when Balaam gives this message: "A Star shall come out of Jacob; a Sceptre shall rise out of Israel" (Numbers 24:17, NKJV). He's talking about Jesus. In Revelation 22:16, Jesus calls Himself the bright morning star. And in Genesis 49:10, Jacob says the ruling sceptre will not depart from Judah until Shiloh comes. The presence of God was at Shiloh in those days, so what he's saying is, someone from Judah's family will rule until God comes to live among His people forever. When every enemy is under Jesus' authority, He'll then hand Himself over to God, who will rule over everything (1 Corinthians 15:28).

I'm happy to have Jesus as King of my life, and to know He'll lead me into God's everlasting kingdom.

6 DECEMBER
God's Mouthpiece
Deuteronomy 18:9-19

"The Lord your God will give you a prophet like me, who is one of your own people. Listen to Him" – Deuteronomy 18:15

Here, Moses writes about when Israel enters their promised land. God is very much against witchcraft, magic, and communicating with the spirits of dead people. "The nations you will force out listen to people who use magic and witchcraft, but the Lord your God will not let you do those things. The Lord your God will give you a prophet like me, who is one of your own people. Listen to Him" (Deuteronomy 18:14-15). As well as telling Israel what not to listen to, God told them who they should listen to ... but who was He talking about?

John the Baptist, son of Jesus' mother's relative Elizabeth, was asked: "Are you the prophet?" (John 1:21), but he answered no. He was a prophet (he gave messages from God), but he wasn't the prophet – the one God had promised to Israel.

Here's something else about this prophet like Moses: "I will tell Him what to say, and He will tell them everything I command. This prophet will speak for Me; anyone who does not listen when He speaks will answer to Me" (Deuteronomy 18:18-19). Do you recognise Him yet?

It might help to know what Jesus said to His followers just before He died. "The words I say to you don't come from Me, but the Father lives in Me and does His own work" (John 14:10).

Once in His earthly life, Jesus was transformed before His friends' eyes. Suddenly, His face shone like the sun and His clothes were dazzling white. Moses and Elijah (who'd lived centuries before) appeared and talked with Him. Peter was overawed by all this, and started waffling on without thinking. He was interrupted by a cloud covering them and God's voice: "This is My Son, whom I love, and I am very pleased with Him. Listen to Him" (Matthew 17:5). Moses and Elijah were important figures in Jewish history, but here God shows that Jesus is above them all.

Jesus is the one we should listen to – an Israelite like Moses, who speaks the very words of God.

7 DECEMBER
Famous Family
Ruth 4:9-12

"May you become powerful in the district of Ephrathah and famous in Bethlehem" – Ruth 4:11

Ruth's a popular story, probably because it's romantic. Initially, Ruth's only connection to Israel is by marriage. There was a famine, so Elimelech and his wife Naomi decided to leave their promised land in favour of Moab, where there was food. They filled their bellies and their sons married Moabite women, but eventually the menfolk died. Naomi returned to her hometown of Bethlehem. Out of loyalty to her mother-in-law, Ruth went with her.

Ruth found work in the fields at harvest time and met a man named Boaz. He was related to Naomi, who thought he'd be a good catch for her daughter-in-law. Israel had a law that the closest relative should marry the wife of the deceased, in order that his name could continue through any child they had. Boaz wanted to do this for Ruth, but ... he wasn't their closest relative!

In Ruth 4, Boaz talks to the leading men of the town. He brings in the closest relative and tells him Naomi's selling her property. Buying it will make him Ruth's husband, but he doesn't want to carry on another man's name! More concerned with his own affairs, he steps aside and lets Boaz do the honours.

When it's all settled, the people speak a blessing over Boaz and Ruth. "May the Lord make this woman, who is coming into your home, like Rachel and Leah, who had many children and built up the people of Israel. May you become powerful in the district of Ephrathah and famous in Bethlehem. As Tamar gave birth to Judah's son Perez, may the Lord give you many children through Ruth. May your family be great like his" (Ruth 4:11-12).

We meet Perez in Genesis 38:27-29 - Boaz's great great great great grandfather (Ruth 4:18-21). Boaz and Ruth had a son Obed, a grandson Jesse, and a great grandson – David. Many centuries later, the most famous son of King David was born – of course, Jesus.

In Matthew 1:5, Ruth's listed in the genealogy of Christ. Her family certainly did become famous in Bethlehem!

8 December
From Small Beginnings
Isaiah 11:1-10

"At that time the new king from the family of Jesse will stand as a banner for all peoples" – Isaiah 11:10

We saw yesterday that Jesse was Boaz and Ruth's grandson. Here in the words of Isaiah, we learn he'll have an ancestor whom God's Spirit will rest upon. This will be someone who finds His delight in obeying God.

When I read the phrase: "With the breath of His lips He shall slay the wicked" (Isaiah 11:4, NKJV), I think of how believing in Jesus' name determines where we'll spend eternity. "We must all stand before Christ to be judged" (2 Corinthians 5:10).

Jesus led the way to God's kingdom by coming into our world as a little child. Thanks to Him we can look forward to a future on God's holy mountain, where nothing will hurt or destroy. A child can reach safely into the nest of a poisonous snake (Isaiah 11:8) because, as Habakkuk also says (Habakkuk 2:14), just as the sea is full of water, the earth will be full of the knowledge of God. Imagine having God's heart inside you, and knowing deep-down what He expects of you. That's the knowledge of God!

"At that time there will be someone special from Jesse's family. He will be like a flag that all the nations gather around. The nations will come to Him and ask Him what they should do. And the place where He is will be filled with glory" (Isaiah 11:10, ERV). Isn't that a lovely picture – all the nations, not just Jews, coming to Jesus for wisdom? It reminds me of what Jesus said to His followers. "God's kingdom is like a mustard seed that a man plants in his field. It is the smallest of all seeds. But when it grows, it is the largest of all garden plants. It becomes a tree big enough for the birds to come and make nests in its branches" (Matthew 13:31-32, ERV).

Let's go to this branch from Jesse's family. Let's shelter in Him, and listen to His advice for us.

9 December
David's Descendant
2 Samuel 7:1-16

"'But your family and your kingdom will continue always before Me. Your throne will last forever'" – 2 Samuel 7:16

We've heard of King David already, but now let's look at some parting words to his son Solomon. He's passing on the promise God made to him in today's reading. "If your descendants live as I tell them and have complete faith in Me, a man from your family will always be king over the people of Israel" (1 Kings 2:4).

Sadly, they didn't always live the way God told them to. Solomon had seven hundred wives and they eventually turned his heart away from God, just as God had warned (1 Kings 11:1-13). That's why Judah separated from the rest of Israel. God was tearing the kingdom away from Solomon's family. He still allowed them to rule over Judah, but it wasn't all smooth-sailing. With a few exceptions, the kings of Judah degenerated, until they were murdering, practising magic, and worshipping false gods (2 Kings 21:3-6).

Remember a few days ago, we saw that God told the Israelites: "The nations you will force out listen to people who use magic and witchcraft" (Deuteronomy 18:14)?

Now His chosen people were in a worse state. He couldn't let it continue, so He said: "I will wipe out Jerusalem as a person wipes a dish and turns it upside-down. I will throw away the rest of My people who are left. I will give them to their enemies" (2 Kings 21:13-14). It must have been a sad day when the ruler of Babylon took Judah away from her country and appointed a governor in place of her king. In the natural run of things, it was inconceivable that a man from David's line could ever reign again.

But when the angel Gabriel visits Mary, he says Jesus will be given the throne of His father David (Luke 1:31-32, NKJV). When human plans fail, God can step in and turn it around. That's what Christians call redemption.

When things seem impossible, God can make them happen – a descendant of David to sit on his throne, just as had been promised.

10 December
A Ruler from Bethlehem
Micah 5:2-5

"'But you, Bethlehem Ephrathah, though you are too small to be among the army groups from Judah, from you will come one who will rule Israel for Me'" – Micah 5:2

Long after David and Solomon, during the time Jotham, Ahaz and Hezekiah were kings in Judah, a man named Micah began to speak for God. He warned of Judah's impending departure from their land, but also looked further into the future. "Jerusalem was hurt and crippled. She was thrown away. She was hurt and punished, but I will bring her back to Me" (Micah 4:6, ERV).

He went on to discuss Bethlehem – a town about six miles from Jerusalem. "But you, Bethlehem Ephrathah, though you are little among the thousands of Judah, yet out of you shall come forth to Me the One to be Ruler in Israel, whose goings forth are from of old, from everlasting" (Micah 5:2, NKJV). From a small, seemingly insignificant town would come a ruler of Israel – a ruler from eternity? That's exactly what the Bible says about Jesus. "In the beginning was the Word, and the Word was with God, and the Word was God. And the Word became flesh and dwelt among us" (John 1:1, 14,

NKJV). Jesus had been with God in the beginning. Thousands of years later, He came to earth in the flesh. Mary and Joseph went to Bethlehem and while they were there, the time came for Mary to give birth (Luke 2:4-7).

Micah doesn't stop there. He wants to say more about this ruler. "The LORD will give up His people until the one who is having a baby gives birth; then the rest of His relatives will return to the people of Israel. At that time the ruler of Israel will stand and take care of His people with the LORD's strength and with the power of the name of the LORD His God. The Israelites will live in safety, because His greatness will reach all over the earth. He will bring peace" (Micah 5:3-5).

This Christmas, let's celebrate that Jesus was born in Bethlehem. Let's play our part in spreading His greatness all over the earth.

11 December
Doorway of Hope
Isaiah 42:1-4

"He will not lose hope or give up until He brings justice to the world. And people far away will trust His teachings" – *Isaiah 42:4*

In Matthew 12, Jesus challenged religious leaders about their priorities and made sick people well. Matthew tells us He did these things to bring about what Isaiah had said, and then he quotes the passage we've just read. "Here is My servant whom I have chosen. I love Him, and I am pleased with Him. I will put My Spirit upon Him, and He will tell of My justice to all people. He will not argue or cry out; no one will hear His voice in the streets. He will not break a crushed blade of grass or put out even a weak flame until He makes justice win the victory. In Him will the non-Jewish people find hope" (Matthew 12:18-21).

I'm reminded of God's words to Hosea. He was talking about when Israel had brought trouble on herself by being disloyal to God, and He said: "I will make the Valley of Trouble a door of hope" (Hosea 2:15) – again, God stepping in and turning things around. I think that's His specialty.

Jesus is the ultimate doorway of hope, because He's the

way for non-Jews to join the Israelites in God's kingdom. "I am the door, and the person who enters through Me will be saved and will be able to come in and go out and find pasture" (John 10:9). Believing in Jesus means we can pray to God through Him. Just like someone might put the kettle on after a busy day to unwind with a cup of tea, through prayer, we can go into heaven and take our day to God for Him to reinvigorate us.

A drink is only temporary, but God's rest and strength are there whenever we need them. It's a privilege to have that kind of access to God in heaven.

12 DECEMBER
Shepherd
Ezekiel 34:11-27

"'Then I will put over them one shepherd, My servant David. He will feed them and tend them and be their shepherd'" - Ezekiel 34:23

I n the eighth year Nebuchadnezzar reigned in Babylon, he imprisoned Jehoiachin - Judah's penultimate ruler before her exile (2 Kings 24:12). Five years later, Ezekiel started to hear from God about a time when all Jerusalem would be captured. As usual, the warnings were interspersed with messages of hope.

In this chapter, God's criticising Israel's leaders for not shepherding His people as they should. "How terrible it will be for the shepherds of Israel who feed only themselves! Why don't the shepherds feed the flock? You have not made the weak strong. You have not healed the sick or put bandages on those that were hurt. You have not brought back those who strayed away or searched for the lost" (Ezekiel 34:2, 4). No food; no healing; no reconciliation. God goes on to say He'll do those very things Himself. "Then I will put over them one shepherd, My servant David. He will feed them and tend them and be their shepherd" (Ezekiel 34:23).

Jesus made it clear He was the Shepherd God spoke about. "I am the good shepherd. I know My sheep, and My sheep know Me, just as the Father knows Me, and I know the Father. I give my life for the sheep. I have other sheep that are not in this flock, and I must bring them also. They will listen to My voice, and there will be one flock and one shepherd" (John 10:14-16).

Jesus sought out people like Zacchaeus (Luke 19:1-10), who would never have talked to Him in person without some encouragement. He cared for those who were hurting, physically or emotionally. I think of the man (in Mark 5:1-20) cutting himself with stones, and how Jesus put an end to his torment. Peter denied knowing Jesus several times, but after Jesus cooked for him and showed him mercy (John 21:9-19), suddenly he was strong and courageous.

What about us? Will we look out only for ourselves, or will we do our best to shepherd and care for people the way Jesus did?

13 DECEMBER
Peace Treaty
Ezekiel 37:21-28

"'I will make an agreement of peace with them, an agreement that continues forever'" – Ezekiel 37:26

Israel and Judah had been separate for generations, but God confided in Ezekiel about bringing them back together (Ezekiel 37:22). God would save them from all the ways they had turned against Him and make them clean. His servant David would be their king, and they would all have one shepherd. I wonder what Ezekiel made of that. A descendant of David was still reigning at that point. Did he think God was referring to the immediate future – that if the people got their act together, perhaps Jerusalem's fall could be prevented?

But God wasn't focused on the here-and-now; He had eternity in mind. "They will all live on the land forever: They, their children, and their grandchildren. David My servant will be their king forever. I will make an agreement of peace with them, an agreement that continues forever. I will put them in their land and make them grow in number. Then I will put My Temple among them forever" (Ezekiel 37:25-26). A time is coming when the old heaven and the old earth will make way for new ones. In the new Jerusalem, there won't be a physical temple; God and Jesus are its temple (Revelation 21:22), and Jesus is the agreement of peace between God and His people. I love how Paul explains it: "But now in Christ Jesus, you who were far away from God are brought near through the blood of Christ's death. Christ Himself is our peace. He made both Jewish people and those who are not Jews one people. They were separated as if there were a wall between them, but Christ broke down that wall of hate by giving His own body" (Ephesians 2:13-14).

Today might be a good day to think about where we stand with God. Do we want to be part of that agreement – have our names written on the peace treaty?

14 DECEMBER
Born of a Virgin
Isaiah 7:1-16

"The virgin will be pregnant. She will have a son, and she will name Him Immanuel" - Isaiah 7:14

Remember Micah's words about a ruler coming from Bethlehem? Isaiah was one of Micah's contemporaries. He spoke to King Ahaz when Aram and Israel joined forces to attack Judah. God reassured Ahaz: "They have made plans against you ... But I, the LORD God, say, 'Their plan will not succeed'" (Isaiah 7:5, 7). He even coaxed him to ask for a sign to prove it.

God does give signs from heaven when it's going to build us up in our faith, but despite the encouragement, Ahaz said: "I will not ask for a sign or test the LORD" (Isaiah 7:12).

Isaiah's not at all impressed. "Isn't it bad enough that you wear out the patience of people? Do you also have to wear out the patience of my God?" God's giving Ahaz a sign, whether he wants one or not. The sign is this: "The virgin will be pregnant. She will have a son, and she will name Him Immanuel" (Isaiah 7:14).

Although this appears unlikely, it takes place. "How will this happen since I am a virgin?" Mary asks when she learns of her upcoming pregnancy, and the angel Gabriel says the Holy Spirit will envelope her (Luke 1:34-35). Mary and Joseph go to Bethlehem because a census is being taken and Bethlehem happens to be Joseph's hometown, and Jesus is born. The timing is perfect. "'She will give birth to a son, and you will name Him Jesus, because He will save His people from their sins.' All this happened to bring about what the LORD had said through the prophet: 'The virgin will be pregnant. She will have a son, and they will name Him Immanuel,' which means 'God is with us'" (Matthew 1:21-23).

Immanuel was a sign to Ahaz, to prove the validity of God's Word. He's the same for us. "I am the way, and the truth, and the life," Jesus says. "The only way to the Father is through Me" (John 14:6).

Jesus came from a virgin's womb, to prove that God is trustworthy and true.

15 December
Spared for a Purpose
Isaiah 61

"The LORD God has put His Spirit in me, because the LORD has appointed me" – Isaiah 61:1

After Jesus was born, some men came to Jerusalem, hoping to worship this King of the Jews. Herod pretended to have the same desire when in reality, he wanted to kill the child to protect his throne.

In Biblical times, distant nations like Babylon had wise men/Magi. That's where we get the word magic from. They were magicians and astrologers – definitely not a lifestyle God wanted for His people, but He didn't toss them aside. Instead, they were an unfolding of God's plan – His kingdom (through Jesus) being made available not just to Jews, but to those from other cultures who came looking. The wise men gave Jesus gold, frankincense and myrrh, and they didn't return to Herod (Matthew 2:11-12).

Once Herod realised they had bypassed him, he gave an order to kill all the boys in Bethlehem under two years of age (Matthew 2:16), but God was one step ahead. He warned Joseph beforehand in a dream, so Joseph took his family to Egypt to escape the slaughter. Hosea talks about

God calling His Son out of Egypt (Hosea 11:1) and after Herod died, they did return to Israel.

For the first time when His life was in danger, Jesus was spared. There would be other times. People attempted to throw Him off a cliff (Luke 4:28-30) or picked up stones to stone Him (John 8:59), but Jesus was spared for a reason, and Isaiah's words we've read today tell us why. He quoted them years later at the synagogue in His hometown. God's Spirit was on Him to preach good news to the poor, to announce freedom for the captives and recovery of sight for the blind (Luke 4:14-21). When God's Spirit is on someone for a particular purpose, it's called being anointed. That's what the words Christ and Messiah mean – Anointed One.

As we think of Jesus being spared, let's celebrate that whatever obstacles seem to hinder God's plan, He's more than able to overcome them. Let's ask God to show us the purpose He has for our lives.

16 DECEMBER
Making His Home
Isaiah 9:1-7

"Before those people lived in darkness, but now they have seen a great light" – Isaiah 9:2

Jesus was born in Bethlehem. When Joseph and the family returned from Egypt, they went to Nazareth, where He was raised. Later, Jesus settled in a different part of Galilee – Capernaum. Remember on day 2, we talked about Abraham's grandson Jacob having twelve sons? Capernaum was in the area originally promised to his sons Zebulun and Naphtali. It was called Galilee of the Gentiles – a place where non-Jews had settled among Jewish people.

The Jews thought of non-Jews (or Gentiles) as unenlightened. They wouldn't even eat with them, as they considered them unclean. However Isaiah turns this on its head, and when Matthew writes about where Jesus lived, he quotes Isaiah's words: "The land of Zebulun and the land of Naphtali, by the way of the sea, beyond the Jordan, Galilee of the Gentiles: The people who sat in darkness have seen a great light, and upon those who sat in the region and shadow of death light has dawned" (Matthew 4:15-16, NKJV). The Gentiles had seen a great light, because Jesus had made His home among them.

The same can be said of us. When we love Jesus, we'll obey His commands, and He and God the Father will come to us and make their home with us (John 14:23). We'll have the Wonderful Counsellor, the Mighty God, an Everlasting Father, the Prince of Peace in our hearts! This comes with some responsibility. Paul tells us: "Let the peace of God rule in your hearts" (Colossians 3:15, NKJV). When we feel anxious or fearful, we can remember the Prince of Peace and allow Him to transform our attitude.

We can celebrate, as the Gentiles could in Jesus' time. Once a people who sat in darkness, they had seen a great light! If we've seen it too and we've asked Him to live inside us, let's be the people He wants us to be.

17 DECEMBER
Light of the World
Isaiah 49:1-6

"'I will make You a light for all nations to show people all over the world the way to be saved'" – Isaiah 49:6

Jesus was given His name when He was eight days old. Several weeks later, Mary and Joseph took Him to a special purification ceremony for mothers of new-borns, which Moses wrote about in Leviticus 12. While they were at the temple, God's Holy Spirit led someone else there – a man named Simeon. He had already promised Simeon he would stay alive until he saw the Christ, so God led him to the temple that day to see Jesus. Holding the child in his arms, Simeon called Jesus 'A light to bring revelation to the Gentiles' (Luke 2:32, NKJV). He was seeing the fulfilment of Isaiah's words. Not only was Jesus someone who would gather Jews and bring them back to God, He was also a light to show Gentiles the way back to Him.

How would He show the way? Simeon had some words for Mary about this, not all of them comforting. "He will be a sign from God that many people will not accept so that the thoughts of many will be made known. And the things that will happen will make your heart sad" (Luke 2:34-35).

Jesus wasn't always accepted. He was eventually sentenced to death and handed over to the Romans to be crucified. He could legitimately have quoted Isaiah from the cross: "I have spent My strength for nothing and in vain, yet surely My just reward is with the LORD" (Isaiah 49:4, NKJV). In human terms, it looked as if it had all been for nothing, but He relied on God for His reward. "He accepted the shame of the cross as if it were nothing because of the joy He could see waiting for Him" (Hebrews 12:2, ERV) – the joy of seeing people once more at-peace with God.

Today we can give thanks that through His death, Jesus has shone a light to show us the way. Will we follow that way to a God-centred life?

18 DECEMBER
Groundwork
Isaiah 40:3-11

"This is the voice of one who calls out: 'Prepare in the desert the way for the Lord'" – Isaiah 40:3

Jesus certainly came to enlighten us, but His light didn't shine out of nowhere. God had planned for it since pre-day one. Before the world began, He had a strategy in mind, and gave us clues along the way. Today's reading is one: The promise of a voice in the wilderness, urging people to prepare for the Lord. John the Baptist was that voice, which came after a time of spiritual wilderness.

Several centuries previously, God had said: "The days are coming when I will cause a time of hunger in the land. The people will not be hungry for bread or thirsty for water, but they will be hungry for words from the LORD" (Amos 8:11). After this, for a period of around four hundred years, nobody heard any messages from God.

Then suddenly, a boy is born to a couple who've been childless for many years. This is John the Baptist, son of Elizabeth – the one the angel told Mary about when he said: "Everyone thought she could not have a baby, but she has been pregnant now for six months. God can do anything" (Luke 1:36-37, ERV).

John the Baptist arrives miraculously. His father's so full of unbelief that God strikes him dumb! Only temporarily though. Imagine the moment Zechariah gets his voice back – the praise that gushes out! What does he say when holding his baby son? "Now you, child, will be called a prophet of the Most High God. You will go before the Lord to prepare His way. You will make His people know that they will be saved by having their sins forgiven" (Luke 1:76-77).

That's exactly what John the Baptist did. He told people about the forgiveness they could experience by believing in Jesus (John 1:29). He made inroads, preparing their hearts for the Lord who was to come.

When God plans, He doesn't do it lightly. He takes time to prepare us and those we associate with. Perhaps something in your life or mine hasn't come about because there's still some unseen work to be done.

19 DECEMBER
Bridegroom
Song of Solomon 5:10-16

"I desire him very much. Yes, daughters of Jerusalem, this is my lover and my friend" – Song of Solomon 5:16

I remember John the Baptist for describing Jesus this way. "The bride belongs to the bridegroom. The friend who attends the bridegroom waits and listens for him, and is full of joy when he hears the bridegroom's voice. That joy is mine, and it is now complete" (John 3:29, NIV). To me, John the Baptist's like a best man, even though I know Jesus doesn't really have favourites.

Today's reading is from Song of Solomon - the Biblical romance between King Solomon and a peasant-woman, which mirrors the love between Jesus and His people. It's full of dialogue, mainly the woman's to her lover and his responses. I like to read the woman's words and imagine I'm saying them to Jesus, or read the responses and think of Him saying them to me. "You have stolen my heart, my sister, my bride" (Song of Solomon 4:9, NIV).

What role does the church have as Jesus' bride? "Wives, yield to your husbands, as you do to the Lord, because the husband is the head of the wife" (Ephesians 5:22-23). It's up to us to accept Jesus' will for our lives – to follow the plans He has for us, rather than go our own way. It's also our responsibility to do the good works God has prepared for us. "'Let us rejoice and be happy and give God glory, because the wedding of the Lamb has come, and the Lamb's bride has made herself ready. Fine linen, bright and clean, was given to her to wear.' (The fine linen means the good things done by God's holy people)" (Revelation 19:7-8).

What about Jesus? What's His role as Bridegroom? "Husbands, love your wives, just as Christ also loved the church and gave Himself for her" (Ephesians 5:25, NKJV). The role of a husband is one of love and self-sacrifice.

How amazing to be so greatly loved by Jesus as to resemble a bride with her groom. I can say with the peasant-woman: "This is my beloved, and this is my friend" (Song of Solomon 5:16, NKJV).

20 December
See the King
Zechariah 9:9-10:4

"Shout for joy, people of Jerusalem! Your King is coming to you. He does what is right, and He saves. He is gentle and riding on a donkey, on the colt of a donkey" - Zechariah 9:9

To know the significance of a life, you have to see it as a whole, so let's concentrate briefly on Jesus' final days on earth. When He entered Jerusalem on a young donkey not yet ridden (Mark 11:2), a crowd met Him. Why? Jesus had befriended a brother and two sisters. The brother died due to illness, but Jesus raised him from the dead! A great number of people witnessed this, and they told others, which is why so many went to meet Jesus (John 12:17-18). How could they not realise what they were seeing?

When Judah returned to their own land after being exiled into Babylon, two men spoke God's messages to them – Haggai, and Zechariah. Zechariah focused greatly on the future and said this. "Shout for joy, people of Jerusalem! Your King is coming to you. He does what is right, and He saves. He is gentle and riding on a donkey, on the colt of a donkey" (Zechariah 9:9). Jesus' followers didn't understand at the time, but later remembered this was written about Him (John 12:16).

If Zechariah 9:9 is about Jesus, the rest of the chapter makes more sense. "The King will talk to the nations about peace ... because of the blood of the agreement with you I will set your prisoners free" (Zechariah 9:10-11). Imprisoned by our wrongdoing, Jesus' blood shed on the cross offered freedom – entry into a new agreement between us and God. "From Judah will come the cornerstone, and the tent peg, the battle bow, and every ruler" (Zechariah 10:4). Like a cornerstone or a tent peg, Jesus holds everything together.

But not everyone that day was prepared to come under His rule. Some wanted Jesus to silence His followers; and when He saw Jerusalem, He wept. "I wish you knew today what would bring you peace. But now it is hidden from you" (Luke 19:42). These words give us a hint of what's to come.

Let's recognise when Jesus does something special in our lives, and let's eagerly praise Him.

21 December
Washed Clean
Isaiah 52:13-53:12

"We all have wandered away like sheep; each of us has gone his own way. But the LORD has put on Him the punishment for all the evil we have done" – Isaiah 53:6

In today's reading, we glimpse Jesus as He grew from babyhood to adulthood – always close to God; a seemingly ordinary man, with no exceptional beauty that would attract us to Him. If anything, at the close of His time on earth, people were appalled by Him. When Isaiah warned of Jesus' death, he called Him a man of sorrows – someone people would look at and mistakenly think He was being disciplined by God. In reality, it was our wrongdoing He was put to death for, not His own.

When Jesus ate a final meal with His friends before He died, as they shared bread and wine together, He said: "This wine represents the new agreement from God to His people. It will begin when My blood is poured out for you" (Luke 22:20, ERV). In other words, all Isaiah's talk about each one of us wandering away like sheep and God laying on Him the punishment for our evil? That pointed to Jesus. His blood shed on that Roman cross was an invitation to us to be washed clean.

Zechariah explained it well. "At that time a fountain will be opened for David's descendants and for the people of Jerusalem to cleanse them of their sin and uncleanness" (Zechariah 13:1). When we identify ourselves as God's people, Jesus' blood is a fountain for us. We come under it (like a fountain of clean, pure water) to have all those terrible things we've said or thought or done washed away, and to experience His forgiveness. That's what you see when a Christian is baptised. They're submerged underwater to symbolise that Jesus' death now covers their faults.

Let's thank God for His offer of forgiveness, and let's consider coming under the fountain of Jesus' blood to experience it for ourselves.

22 December
The Pain of Victory
Isaiah 63:1-9

"'I have walked in the winepress alone, and no one among the nations helped Me'" – Isaiah 63:3

This beautiful passage paints a picture in my mind of what Jesus went through for us. Judas Iscariot, one of the twelve people closest to Jesus, went to the religious leaders and got a reward of thirty pieces of silver for handing Him over to them (Matthew 26:14-16, NKJV). In the middle of the night in the garden of Gethsemane, Judas greeted Jesus with what looked like a kiss of friendship - the signal for them to arrest Him. Just hours earlier, Judas shared a special meal with Jesus. He listened when Jesus said someone would betray Him and everyone had questioned who it might be (Matthew 26:21-25, NKJV). As Obadiah wrote: "Those who eat your bread will lay a trap for you. No one is aware of it" (Obadiah 1:7).

Judas wasn't the only one to let Jesus down. Mark 14:50 tells us all His followers left Him and ran away, which confirmed Zechariah's message that a Shepherd would be struck and the sheep would scatter (Zechariah 13:7). Peter denied he even knew Jesus, and those were just His friends!

Why spend so much time with flawed humanity? Why go through all that pain? The book of Hebrews says Jesus learnt obedience through His suffering and that because His obedience was perfect, He can save all those who follow Him (Hebrews 5:8-9). If Jesus had taken any shortcuts, if He had called down an army of angels to set Him free (as Matthew 26:53 says He could have), His obedience would have been flawed. He couldn't have been our Saviour.

Let's thank God for Jesus' willingness to put our welfare above His own comfort and convenience.

23 DECEMBER
Undying Love
Psalm 22:1-26

"LORD, I praise You in the great meeting of Your people; these worshippers will see me do what I promised" – Psalm 22:25

Yesterday, we saw how Jesus was betrayed and deserted by His friends. After His arrest came further brutality. As He awaited trial, the guards blindfolded Him and slapped His face. Then they taunted Him: "Prove that you are a prophet, and tell us who hit you" (Luke 22:64). As one-third of the trinity, Jesus was instrumental in creating the whole universe and knew everything. It must have been so tempting to answer! I probably would have, but "As a sheep before its shearers is silent, so He opened not His mouth" (Isaiah 53:7, NKJV).

Then there were the soldiers, twisting a crown of thorns for His head and saying derisively: "Hail, King of the Jews!" (Mark 15:16-20). Jesus was badly-beaten - His appearance so damaged, He didn't look like a man (Isaiah 52:14). One changed his tune later, but initially both men crucified alongside Jesus insulted Him (Matthew 27:44).

The words of Psalm 22 are fitting: "All those who see me ridicule me" (V7, NKJV). Jesus even quoted the Psalm

Himself: "My God, My God, why have You abandoned Me?" (V1). Affixed as He was to the cross, all His bones must have been out of joint, and they pierced His hands and feet (Vs14-16). The soldiers also did exactly what it said and gambled for His clothing (V18). After Jesus died, another Psalm came true when a soldier pierced His side instead of breaking His legs. Psalm 34:20 said none of His bones would be broken.

God allowed Jesus to endure it all. We've touched on the fact He wanted to save us, but why was that so important? John famously gives us the answer. "God loved the world so much that He gave His only Son" (John 3:16, ERV). Jesus' love will go to these lengths, just for us. What's more, if we receive His love, it can be ours forever.

As we consider the legacy Jesus left, let's remember the reason for it all - an unwavering love for you and me. Why don't we respond by loving Him back?

24 DECEMBER
The Full Story
Psalm 16

"You will not leave me in the grave. You will not let Your holy one rot" – Psalm 16:10

It's Christmas Eve, and Advent is almost over. We've looked at Jesus' life and seen how so many of God's promises were realised in Him ... but we can't finish with His death, because that's not the end of the story.

Psalm 16:10 says God won't leave His holy One in the grave. Jesus' friend Peter explains in Acts 2:25-31 that David wasn't referring to himself, because David's body is dead and buried; he was talking about the Christ.

Three days after He hung on that awful, bloodied cross, Jesus' friends looked into an empty tomb. Jesus wasn't there! God had raised Him from the dead! Jesus already explained that God was the God of the living, not the dead (Matthew 22:32), so how can we follow a dead leader? It has to be someone who lives.

Jesus said it was to our advantage that He was going to the Father, because then He would send the Holy Spirit (John 16:7-11, ERV). That's why Christians can have such a vibrant faith. If Jesus hadn't been raised to life and His Spirit couldn't live in us, our faith would be useless.

When we tell the story of Jesus, we can tell it in full. It's not just about someone who was born, or who died for us. It's about someone who's very much alive, with the power to transform people and situations. As a follower of Jesus, His Spirit lives in your heart, giving you access to God and everything He has for you.

The end of the story is, there isn't really an end. Our lives are the next chapter.

25 DECEMBER
Joy for All
Psalm 45:1-11

"God has chosen you from among your friends; He has set you apart with much joy" – Psalm 45:7

This Psalm (my favourite Psalm, actually) talks about a king who's been earmarked by joy. It seems appropriate to think about joy today. All those promises God made, all those years of waiting, and finally the day came: Jesus was born, and the angel brought good news to those shepherds – a great joy to all the people – Christ, the Lord (Luke 2:10-11).

The last part of today's reading is a good reminder to us, however we spend our Christmas. "Because He is your Lord, worship Him" (Psalm 45:11, NKJV). If we're celebrating with loved ones, we can worship Jesus by treating them with kindness, as He Himself would treat them. If we're on our own, we can worship Him by acknowledging that we'll never be totally alone. When Matthew explained how the birth of Jesus came about (Matthew 1:18-25), he said they would name Him Immanuel, which means "God is with us".

As you think back over this book and all that has come to pass because of Jesus, may it be an encouragement to you that whatever God says, He'll make it happen. "But for you who revere My name, the sun of righteousness will rise with healing in its rays. And you will go out and frolic like well-fed calves" (Malachi 4:2, NIV). Charles Wesley captured this verse in a well-known carol:

Hail the heavenly Prince of Peace! Hail the Sun of Righteousness! Light and life to all He brings!

Happy Christmas.

Printed in Poland
by Amazon Fulfillment
Poland Sp. z o.o., Wrocław

63395134R00034